ABINGDON'S
Easter
Recitations

Compiled by
Evelyn Minshull

ABINGDON PRESS
Nashville

CONTENTS

The plays, songs, and recitations found in this collection mirror the contrasting moods of the first Holy Week—the expectation of Palm Sunday, the betrayal of Holy Thursday, the shock and depression of Good Friday, the exultant joy of Easter.

This collection is not meant to provide prepackaged programs but to be a springboard from which you can launch many meaningful, personalized Holy Week celebrations. Blend these materials with others you select or develop; choose music and scriptures that crystallize the meaning of Holy Week for your group.

To assist the director, scriptures and supplemental music are suggested. Recitations are keyed for probable age levels as follows:

B—beginner   **P**—primary   **I**—intermediate
J—junior   **T**—teen   **A**—adult

THE PARADE OF PALMS

A Pageant for Palm Sunday

Children in biblical costume come romping in, thumping tambourines, and playing other such rhythm instruments. They move quickly, turn often, raise their arms at times, and smile. One asterisk in the following recitation indicates a slight pause and a definite beat of maracas and tambourines; two asterisks mean two quick beats.

Pageant: **The Parade of Palms** (*I*)

> Gather up your neighbors! Raise your voice in psalms!
> Join the celebration—the parade * * of palms!
> Smile at perfect strangers! Give a beggar alms!
> It's a time for sharing—the parade * * of palms!
> (*rhythm changes*)
> Everyone loves a parade * *
> Everyone loves a parade *
> And this one is special; this one is fine—
> designed to honor a friend of mine!
> Jesus is coming to town * *
> Jesus is coming to town!
> So-o-o-o-o-o-o-o * (*rhythm resumes*)

ALL: Come along and join us—even dads and moms!
Join the celebration—the parade * * of palms!

Children rush forward and pantomime actions suggested in this recitation.

Recitation: **Hurry, Hurry!** (*J or group of I*)

SPEAKER 1: Hurry, hurry to the palm tree; reaching, stand on tippy-toe.
Palm fronds rattle far above you—as they rustle, as they blow.

2: Climbing up, small knees are bleeding;
closer, now—an inch or so.
Still, the stems are tough and stubborn.
Tug and pull; they won't let go.

3: Hear the people shout hosanna! Hear the shouts along the way.
Sad to miss the wild excitement of this very special day.

4: Scramble down, the rough bark tearing;
run and stumble; heartbeats pound.
Peer between the knees and ankles;
garments lie there, on the ground.

5: He is coming! He is coming! Hear the glad hosannas rise!
Now peer up past donkey's hoofbeats;
look into the Savior's eyes.

6: Sad—no palm branch to be waving;
still, you have the greater part.
You can sing and shout hosannas.
You may offer him your heart!

All except a few of the hymns and carols suggested throughout this collection can be found in one or more of these hymnals: *The Book of Hymns* (The United Methodist Publishing House, 1964, 1966); *The Methodist Hymnal* (The Methodist Publishing House, 1932, 1935, 1939); and *All-American Church Hymnal* (John T. Benson Publishing Co.).

Receding to background, the children wave their palm branches and look expectantly offstage. A modern child, looking morose, comes forward—hands in pockets, shoulders slumped—and recites.

Recitation: **I've Looked and Looked and Looked** (*I*)

> I've looked and looked and *looked* and couldn't find one—
> not in the park or in the city square.
> I checked the backyards all around the playground;
> I couldn't find a palm tree anywhere!

A second group of children with party hats and noisemakers march down the right outside aisle; another group of children with various kinds of rhythm instruments move down the left aisle. Still another group with huge bunches of helium-filled balloons come down the center aisle. The speaker watches as they intermingle and march around and around inside the church. The children in biblical costume continue the pageant with building excitement.

ALL: He's coming! Hosanna!
> He's coming; He's coming!
> Our Savior is coming today!

Excitement mounts to greatest pitch, musical instruments sound, light brightens, palm branches are thrown into the air, and balloons are released.

SPEAKER: But who needs a palm branch to bring such a message!
> Jesus, our Savior, is Lord! He is King!
> "Hosanna! Hosanna!" we shout as we greet him.
> I don't need a palm branch to sing!

Song: "Hosanna" (*canon in four parts*)

Recitation: **See Him Riding** (*P*)

> See him riding on a donkey! Hear the people sing and shout!
> Jesus Christ is Lord forever! Who could ever, ever doubt?

Recitation: **For Palm Sunday** (*I*)

> On the day that Jesus rode to town
> the way was crowded, up and down.
> People lined the busy street
> and spread palm branches at his feet.
> The watchers waved. He smiled at them
> as he journeyed to Jerusalem.
> And everyone who saw him cried,
> "Hosanna," as they watched him ride
> upon a donkey's back that day.
> They knew a king had come their way.   *Jean Conder Soule*

5

Recitation: **This Palm Branch I Hold**   (B)

This palm branch I hold means a marvelous thing—
Jesus is Savior—Jesus is king!

Scripture: John 12:12-15

Recitation: **Palm Sunday Tribute**   (T/A)

Jesus rode into Jerusalem
to the welcoming cheers
    of the city's multitudes,
in majestic dignity,
astride an ass.

From thence he moved
straight to the desolation
    of the cross,
the jeers of the crowds accompanying him—
His majesty enhanced,
His dignity unaffected.   *Frederick W. Kemper*

Song: "I Saw a King Today"

Recitation: **Two Points**   (T/A)

The road from the city gates
to Golgotha
may be measured in meters.
    One estimates the space
    from "hosanna"
    to "crucify him"
    in attitudes.
Love is the measure unit
from the taut line
between the triumphal entry
and the crucifixion.
From unfaith to faith
is one blind leap
to sight.   *Frederick W. Kemper*

Scripture: Mark 11:1-11
Suggested Hymns: "Hosanna, Loud Hosanna," "Ride On, Ride On in
                    Majesty"
Song: "Hosanna" (*repeat four-part canon*)

*Children hold placards that spell hosannas. As each speaker delivers a line, the proper
placard is advanced slightly. Children act quickly with excitement.*

6

Recitation: **Acronym** (*J*)

H —— Happy children chatter as they breathe a bright excitement;
O —— Obstinate, they struggle to tug down the palms for pulling;
S —— Satisfied, with branches freed, they run to line the pathway;
A —— Awkwardly, they wave their palms and lean far out to see him.
N —— Never has a king so humbly ridden to his people;
N —— Never on a donkey has a king received such homage!
A —— All along the pathway lie the cloaks of those who praise him;
S —— Surely now begins a Kingdom built on love and justice!

ALL: Hosanna! Shout hosanna! He is come to free his people!
Hosanna! Praise the Savior! He will rule our hearts forever!

Song: "Come, Praise and Sing Hosanna!"

Return to parade formation. Again asterisks indicate pauses and beats of rhythm instruments.

Pageant: **The Parade of Palms, Part B** (*I*)

Isn't it exciting; how could anyone be calm? *
It's a time for singing—the parade * * of palms!
Gather up your neighbors! Raise your voice in psalms!
Join the celebration—the parade * * of palms!

All exit with accompaniment of rhythm instruments. When all is quiet, congregation sings reverently.

Hymn: "All Glory, Laud and Honor"

A NIGHT OF BETRAYALS

Resources for a Holy Thursday Service

The monologue and play included here may be used in a number of ways. Either or both might form the nucleus of a Holy Thursday Service or be used as part of an observance that encompasses Holy Week in its totality. Adult groups might find either a basis for discussion. Choose from music and scriptures suggested below.

Hymns: " 'Tis Midnight," "Go to Dark Gethsemane," "Into the Woods My Master Went"
Song: "Bitter"
Scriptures: Matthew 26:31-35, 69-75; Mark 14:29-30, 66-72; Luke 22:31-34, 54b-62; John 18:25-27; Matthew 26:47-50; Mark 14:10-11; Luke 22:3-6, 17-22, 45-48

Monologue: **I, Judas, Betrayer of a Friend** *(T/A)*

Clammy—the dark, dank wind which claws the slope, raking the grass to ridges as I climb; coldly impersonal—those stars that once drew close, merging their light with lights of heart and mind; maddening my nostrils—scents of loam and bud, precious in youth; reminder now of death. Decay. Reduction of all life to carrion.

Rough in my hands—this rope, shaped to a sailor's purposes, but warped to mine, as all the richness of my textured years has rotted, frayed; as pulsing promises have curdled in my breast since that first turning.

Warm in my palm—the touch where thirty coins were welcomed, nourished—ere I flung them jangling, ringing— *O God! I hear them still!* (*Slight pause to gain control*)

I pierce the flesh to blood—my blood, soon to congeal in self-inflicted death—this cursed blood, coursing through cankered veins which feed these organs—limbs—which implemented death to truth (if truth it was). How that blood surged and sang when I was chosen one of twelve; how it pounded in its pride when I was trusted with our funds, however meager—how it pulsed against those close-felt coins—my spirit doomed already as I acquiesced to details of my villainy. (*Pause, then, with longing*)

Lord, how remembrance crowds these final moments! How sweet life seemed when childhood fancy led me to some sweet swell of slope. Would God I'd spent my life in some far corner where, unknowingly, I'd miss the pulse, the beat of Jewish prophecy, unfolding. Would God I'd known no ardor of his teaching—known no camaraderie of men on fire with passion for this new salvation—but passed the time in placid passiveness—or drudgery—or prisoned dark insanity—safe from the dark responsibility of what I've done.

(*A longer pause, dispassionate, now*) The crest is gained. My breath congeals in strands as I survey the setting for my death—a grove of olive trees to make my rope. But, no, a stream of moonlight proves them small, vibrant with supple, healthy limbs and leafing. Beyond, a snag, mastlike and bare—a monument to ancient death and long unstirring sap—fitting to bear such loathsome weight as mine—casts shadows to the stars.

The stars escape to darkness, and I move more slowly—my feet made heavy by the lead of fears. The night my enemy—there is no deeper dark than in this hollow heart—haunted by all those writhing wraiths of joy and promise which bloomed so briefly, so exuberantly, on our dim horizons. God, how I loved this man, your Son (if Son he is). Swept by the sorcery of soft and silken words of peace which seemed at one with sun and lapping waters on the pebbled sand, I could believe his kinship. But—when I sat, often alone, counting the flickering demons of the fire—feeling the touch of cold on shoulders (that frigid touch of doubt)—I knew—as I know now (or think I know) that he is man, not god—though, *God!* Despite his sweet deception or confusion, I love him still—and hate the very limbs and bowels and tendons of this loathsome self of mine—his dark betrayer.

We were so close, so very close, sharing the stars, the sop, the dust, the rain, the heat—the aching back, the throbbing, blistered feet—the glow when crowds accepted and adored; the pain, the fear, when he was threatened or abused.

8

Oh, yes, I love him—though I see now (or think I see) a few all-human chinks in that perfection we assumed as Godship. He has no head for finance, certainly. Though I adored him, often I fought impatience at his waste, as when the foolish Mary poured such costly ointment to head and hands and feet. The poet in him, surely it was that, transformed that simple wasteful act to one of service, and—while the spikenard gurgled to the floor of Simon's house—I pondered how we needed more a horde of coins than ointment, dissipating in the fragrant air. No world for poets, this—where evil lurks and coils itself to strike, where sunlight flickers 'cross the nests of asps—and kiss of friendship masks a venomous intent.

(*With added tension and despair*) What matters it if he be God—or rogue—or blasphemer? *He was my friend!*

(*A pause, then beginning with quiet despair*) And I remember other hills and other skies where clouds held moving images which brought me peace—and grass—tall, waving, green—invited me to rest my body there and close my eyes while winds, like loving hands, caressed me.

No more! No more! These grasses slash my flesh; these creepers tangle; this ground itself repels and chastens me—the edge of chasm merges with the earth, testing discernment, that I might plunge before decision's firm—to swoop in flailing desperation—moments too soon—to hell. Should not the lights that mark Jerusalem litter the night where Hinnom Valley rises from its depths? Surely the night conspires to hide even the slightest light to ease my darkness. And when I dangle lifelessly from stretched-taut rope, swaying and turning like some limp-rolled sail on drifting vessel—if men should cut me loose and cover me with clods—perhaps the earth itself will heave with loathing and spew me forth again—fit food for vultures.

O God! O God! This life withholds its light and peace from me—and heaven denies the slightest breath of hope—and hell—can hell itself abide the husk, the kernel, of such a blighted ear? Oh, for the warmth of just one human hand to touch mine gently. Oh, for the sweet acceptance of another's eyes, or recognition from *some* eye, even in condemnation. But all the hosts of my accusers are within, waggling their crippled fingers; and in this darksome, chilling night enclosing me—as through the unseen gulf careening from this cliff—there are no terrors which can match for threat the thoughts which swarm—bringing my clamped-tight lids such images of woe which surely hell could never equal—the sounds which throng my ears—that damned, eroding, ceaseless din of silver clinking—then cascading, cast to temple stone, and jingling, jangling, ringing with a din which sharply echoes in each creaking bough, and clatters in the click of sole to stone, and overrides the silver sound of gentle brook.

Echoing down the corridors of mind, those shekels clang and click and move against each other—and apart—winking seductively their silver song. Not all the silver—no, nor all the gold—confined in guarded coffers here and in those unknown kingdoms of the world—nor all the metal yet unmined from bowels of rock or sea—could ransom this dead soul from chains of torment, or purchase peace of mind or soothing sweet forgetfulness.

(*Suddenly, with resolve*) Then let's have done! "That which you do, do quickly," Jesus said, and this I do. See how the amputated limb of lifeless snag bends to my coiling rope. Fumbling, my fingers bind the knots at limb, at neck. I see no sky, no cloud, no verdant hill, no chasm, yawning just beyond my feet. I feel no chill of breeze, and, startlingly, the panic of this endless night congeals with my intent.

Coldly, the warped, accusing demons circulate more dimly, now; coagulated loathings ebb and swell like tides compelling some small craft to port, if snag were mast, and rope coiled to intended tasks, and I a traveler treading wave and foam to some eventual hope.

More dimly, now—the rope drawn taut, my body lifting—the cold cacophony of clinking coins precedes me—into—hell.

The Denial of Peter

(a play for teens and adults)
by Katherine K. Antonson

Characters: Peter, Bartholomew, guard at the palace of Caiaphas, palace servant, Seceel, Woman

Setting: *This play, designed for the chancel of a church, is set in the courtyard of Caiaphas. Elevated slightly, in center stage, is a small artificial fire. Stage left is an area designated as a porch. The center aisle serves as an approach to the courtyard. Stage is empty, except for the fire.* Peter *and* Bartholomew *advance slowly down center aisle, stopping midway to talk.*

BARTH:	Simon Peter, I am tired. Let us stay among these olive trees and rest awhile (*gestures toward trees*). Surely nothing will happen to our Teacher in these dark hours. Caiaphas himself needs sleep and will await the morrow to begin proceedings against our Lord.
PETER:	Be strong, Bartholomew. Already we have wronged our friend enough tonight. We cannot leave him now when he needs our reassuring presence.
BARTH:	It's true, I know.
PETER:	Count up the times we fell asleep in dark Gethsemane. Three times he bade us watch and pray, and three we fell asleep. How could it be that all of us denied him? I did not believe him, when at the table, he announced I would deny him thrice. Already, in the garden, has that prophecy fulfilled itself.
BARTH:	But Peter, in the garden, you were the only one who struck out to save our Lord. You took a step, and with your sword you severed the soldier's ear.
PETER:	It was rash, irresponsible. As quickly as the ear was split, Jesus' hand was held to heal it. Then softly he spoke those rebuking words: "All who take the sword will perish by the sword." Those words, though soft, struck harsh.

10

BARTH:	We acted rasher still, tonight! We fled our Teacher in his hour of need. We ran away, leaving him alone to face the company of soldiers.
PETER:	That is the reason we cannot leave him now. We must hasten to the palace of the priest to see what will happen.
BARTH:	If only God would take away this gnawing fear inside my heart. My body trembles at the thought of even two steps closer to Caiaphas.
PETER:	You're no more fearful than I. I force my legs to walk. And yet we must. We only need to wait within the courtyard, far below the rooms. No one will recognize our faces there.
BARTH:	But what about the servants who will doubtless be around?
PETER:	It's late. Perhaps they'll be in bed. But we must hurry, before they transfer Jesus to another house without our knowledge.

They continue down the aisle, hugging themselves as though cold. Suddenly, Bartholomew *points.*

BARTH:	Look ahead. A fire in the yard, with no one near. What chance! At least our prayer is answered. The chill that fills the night will soon be driven from our bodies.
PETER:	A prayer of praise and thanks be raised—more for the solitude. I worried that our Galilean garb and tongue would easily betray us.
BARTH:	(*Interrupting, pointing to a spot just right of center stage, not visible to the audience*) Peter! Look! The second-story porch. That's Jesus between those guards. They're taking him into a room which fronts the courtyard. We are in luck. We'll know exactly what transpires here tonight.

A door slams offstage.

PETER:	Let us kneel next to the fire. If anyone approaches, we will keep to ourselves. We shall begin our evening's vigil.

They approach the fire and, kneeling, begin to warm themselves. Loud talking and laughing are heard offstage right. Enter guard *and* servant, *who have drunk quite heavily. They are loud, aggressive, obviously pleased with the night's events. Talking, they stand to the right of the fire, and do not notice the two disciples, who grow increasingly tense during their conversation.*

GUARD:	And did you see the guilty one as you took the evening meal into the room? Tell me how he looked.
SERVANT:	Certainly not as I thought he would. He's smaller than they say, and rather homely, dusty, disheveled, but quite calm. He did not look the part he plays.

GUARD:	No revolutionary looks as he should these days. They're well disguised. (*Both laugh*) The high priest— Describe *his* looks to me.
SERVANT:	He fairly gloated in the hall, like one who knows he's won the game. He could not keep a smile from his lips. It's only moments, now, until the man is charged with heresy. Here, have a drink; my gourd is full.
GUARD:	Caiaphas should be well pleased. His plot is nearly completed.
SERVANT:	And it has not been easy to fulfill. In fact, without the aid of Judas Iscariot, the soldiers still would be at a loss to find the man.
GUARD:	This Judas, who is he?
SERVANT:	Some sniveling man who called himself disciple of the guilty one. For thirty silver coins, he sold his friend to bondage. He led the soldiers to Gethsemane, and, with a kiss, betrayed his friend.
GUARD:	More friends should be like that. 'Twould not take long for Caiaphas to squelch rebellion. (*Laughs*)
SERVANT:	Do not think lightly of the high priest. When this Jesus is hung upon the tree, it will be a warning to them all. And no disciple will be safe from that same fate. Have you seen a crucifixion?
GUARD:	Aye—it's not a pretty sight!
SERVANT:	This one's to be worse. Instead of binding up the arms and body to the cross, I hear rumors that they'll *nail* the palms instead—and the feet. A bloody warning to the few remaining faithful.
GUARD:	This death should ruin anarchy for sure. *I'd* not be one to risk such death by crucifixion.
	A pretty girl, the maid Seceel, *appears through an entrance by the porch. She holds a tambourine and shakes it rhythmically as she enters. It seems to be a dance step. When she sees the two men, she walks to the fire, crossing behind* Peter *and* Bartholomew, *who are still sitting nervously.*
SECEEL:	Here you are! I should have searched the courtyard first! The night's festivities have just begun. The song and dance fill up the servants' hall, and here you stand. (*Shakes tambourine, stamps her feet, again, as though part of a dance step*)
GUARD:	Seceel, come here and hear the news our friend has.
	Seceel *advances.*
SERVANT:	Caiaphas has caught the Nazarene. He's being questioned now, above—in private rooms. Think, Seceel, what that will mean!

SECEEL:	(*Thoughtful a moment, then excited*) Caiaphas is sure to have a promotion and a feast will follow and we *all* can celebrate. His bounty will exceed his merriment, and all of us will profit in the bargain and—perhaps—there'll be a reward for each disciple we can catch. (*Playfully, swaggers toward the porch*) I'll take two. (*Crossing back*) But, come— Why dream of the future when festivities await us in the hall? (*Whirls, shaking her tambourine*)
GUARD:	Yes, let's follow. I'm thirsty for an evening's entertainment. (*Crosses toward the entrance Seceel used, turns and waits*)
SERVANT:	(*Calls to guard*) A moment, there! Perhaps these travelers here would care to join us in the song.
GUARD:	I'll go to the hall and tell them we are coming. (*Exits*)
	Servant *moves to right of the disciples. They rise, uncertainly.* Seceel *shakes tambourine and moves to left. They ring the fire;* Bartholomew *is farthest upstage.* Seceel *is looking carefully at* Peter.
SERVANT:	Please pardon our unfriendliness. We did not mean disfavor by ignoring you, but we were caught in a frenzy. No doubt you've heard of Jesus' capture. They say all the city knows.
PETER:	We've heard. (*Tries to turn his back to Seceel who keeps staring at him*)
SERVANT:	It will be a day of feasting when they find him guilty. They're searching even now for witnesses to prove him so.
PETER:	We, too, await the verdict.
SECEEL:	(*Suddenly excited*) I *knew* I knew this man. Come closer to the fire—let me look. (*Pulls Peter closer to the fire*) He's one of them! I saw him in the marketplace two days ago with the accused man. He's a disciple!
	Peter *and* Bartholomew *are terrified.* Peter *seems to take hold of himself. He steps toward* Seceel.
PETER:	You wrong me. (*Pauses, thinking*) I have just this day come to Jerusalem.
SECEEL:	Impossible. I saw you there myself. You were talking to the Nazarene.
PETER:	(*Frustrated, jocular, unconvincing*) Woman, I—I do not know the man.
	Totally surprised by this response, Bartholomew takes Peter by the elbow. Peter shakes him off.
PETER:	Two days ago, my friend and I were on the road from—from Selecah. We were not near Jerusalem.
SECEEL:	He lies! I saw this man with my own eyes.

13

SERVANT:	(*Pulling Seceel to right of fire*) Be wise, Seceel, if he were a disciple to Jesus, why would he be here? So quickly to be found? Surely you mistake him.
SECEEL:	(*Angry at her friend's disbelief*) I'm right. I have a witness. We were together at the market, seeking cloth. I will get her now and prove I am in truth. (*Crosses hurriedly to left exit*)
SERVANT:	(*Going to Peter and Bartholomew, speaks levelly, but seems embarrassed by the girl's behavior*) You must forgive my friend. She is strong in will, not easily put off. This is not hospitality for two who've traveled the distance that you have come. Why don't you join us in the hall? We'll bring some cool refreshments to relax your limbs. (*Draws Peter toward porch*)
PETER:	(*Seeing this as opportunity to leave; sounding offended*) No, our thanks to you. But we do not feel welcome here. We do not wish to intrude upon your evening song. Come, good friend. (*Waves Bartholomew to exit down center aisle*)
	Bartholomew *moves right, but as* Peter *is about to leave the porch area, the* women *burst in, followed by the* guard. *The* women *surround* Peter. *The* men *stand off.*
SECEEL:	See! Here is the man. Is he not the one who accompanied the cursed one in the marketplace?
WOMAN:	In truth! It is. His clothes, the same, his face—in fact, he was called *Peter.* Truly I remember it. *Peter!*
SECEEL:	Yes, that is his name.
PETER:	(*Breaking away, walking downstage*) You are mistaken, both of you. You have not seen my face nor heard my name before. Furthermore, I—I say again, *I do not know the man.*
	Bartholomew *hears the second denial. His body tenses. He steps toward* Peter, *saying,* "Peter—," *then breaks off and turns away. The* guard, *becoming interested, steps to left of* Peter.
GUARD:	They say you are a traveler—from Selecah. You have been long in travel?
PETER:	(*Hesitantly, becoming nervous and anxious*) Perhaps a fortnight. We've stopped along the way to visit friends.
GUARD:	Your accent— Are you native to Selecah? It seems your speech is Galilean. The guilty one had followers from Galilee. Could you—
PETER:	(*His emotion at the highest peak*) The Devil be upon you! I swear by holy heavens that I am not the man you think! I swear by *God* I do *not know the man!*
BARTH:	(*Rushing to Peter*) Peter!
	Offstage, the cock crows. A door slams on the upper porch. Peter *and* Bartholomew *freeze. Both* women *look to see what is happening.* Seceel *points excitedly to the figure who is not seen.*

14

SECEEL:	Look! There is the revolutionist. They must be finished with the trial. See how he's flanked by guards.
WOMAN:	Yes. That's the man we saw when we were shopping in the marketplace. That is the man *Peter* says he does not know.
BARTH:	(*Grasping Peter's shoulders, gently trying to turn him to face Jesus*) Peter, *look* at him. One look will grant forgiveness.
SECEEL:	He stands so still. What holds his rapt attention thus?
BARTH:	Peter—think of all the times he forgave a weary soul who merely looked at him, or touched the hem of his robe. *There is a pause. Slowly,* Peter *turns his body in the direction of the upper porch. He leans on* Bartholomew, *tightly grasping his arm.*
PETER:	Jesus? (*Speaks quietly but with intense lamentation*) Jesus Lord. Can you hear me? I am sorry for my sins. Forgive my soul. (*Turns and rushes back up the center aisle*) Seceel, *seeing him leave, takes a few steps in pursuit, then stops.*
SECEEL:	He's gone! Our one disciple fled afoot!
SERVANT:	He's mad, Seceel. Let us waste no time with him.
SECEEL:	But he is a disciple of Jesus.
SERVANT:	There's plenty time for him. Once Jesus is condemned we will have our chance to look for disciples. Come, let's make merry ere the night is fully gone.
GUARD:	Aye! Let's go to the hall before the songs have stopped and all the wine is drunk. *They exit noisily, laughing.* Bartholomew *is alone on stage. Walking to the opposite corner, he looks up to where Jesus had stood, then out to the audience as he speaks introspectively.*
BARTH:	Jesus, Lord. We drank the cup of wine tonight around the table in the upper room. You said it was your blood, a covenant, which gave to all forgiveness of sin. But it is not only Peter who needs such love this eventide. He is just the one who made denial openly. Yet all of us who are your disciples, Lord, every one of us left you in the garden, and are not doing anything to help you now, every one of us is guilty of denial—and needs forgiveness in the Father's eye. Forgive us all, dear Lord. Forgive us all. (*Exits slowly, head bowed*)

Recitation: **Foot Washers** (*can be used in Holy Thursday Service*)

If Christ, the Master, stoops to wash our feet,
can we love less?   *Frederick W. Kemper*
Scripture: John 13:1-17, 34

Other materials that can be used in this service are: "Ecce Homo," page 16; "I Do Not Know," page 16; "Jesus, Friend of Sinners," page 19; "Easter Breakthrough," page 22; "The Human Prospect," page 22; "A Prayer," page 23.

15

IT IS FINISHED

Resources for a Good Friday Program

Recitation: **Question** (*T/A*)

> It is said
> that the servant is not greater than the master.
> What does one say
> when the Master is the servant?   *Frederick W. Kemper*

Scripture: Isaiah 53

Recitation: **Ecce Homo** (*T/A*)

> Look we for another?
> Where, then, shall we look?
> We are in his fishnet; we are on his hook;
> we are caught securely
> in his shepherd's crook.
>
> Have we been forsaken? Was he not forsook?
> Ridicule we've taken? Think what Jesus took!
> Look we for another?
> We've no need to look.   *Andrew T. Roy*

Scriptures: Select those related to Good Friday
Song: "Lord, Why Me?"

Recitation: **I Do Not Know** (*J/T*)

> I do not know—I cannot tell
> why he should brave the gates of hell
> for me—for me, his weakest friend.
>
> I only know that once he died
> to kill my sins and stem the tide
> of guilt—of guilt that prisoned me.
>
> Now I am free; he paid the price
> with his own life—God's sacrifice
> of love—of love that ransomed me.   *Andrew Stallsmith*

Hymns: "Alas! and Did My Savior Bleed," "Were You There?"

Recitation: **Golgotha** (*J/T/A*)

> Yes, I was there that fateful day
> the day they took our Christ away
> to that dark hill of pain.

16

My sin increased the pain he bore
made sharp the crown of thorns he wore
and drove the nails home.
"Father, forgive them," now he prays.
The dying sun extends its rays
to touch his anguished face.
"Forgive them"—from his loving heart
streams of grace and mercy start
to overcome the world.
Yes, I was there the day he died.
My sin with him was crucified
and I am ever his.   *Andrew Stallsmith*

Hymn: "There Is a Green Hill Far Away"

Recitation: **Lifted Up** (*T/A*)

"As Moses lifted up the serpent in the wilderness, even so must the Son of man be lifted up" (John 3:14 KJV).

God in human flesh:
Immanuel
Perfect flesh; now torn
And violated.
   God—come down to us
   In seeking love
   Now lifted up by us
   In agony.
We look upon him
And he draws
The poison from the serpent's sting,
Heals us, and makes us whole.   *Andrew Stallsmith*

Hymn: "O Sacred Head, Now Wounded"

Recitation: **Finished** (*T/A*)

"It is finished."
From the lips of him made sin for me
that last victorious cry announced to all the universe
that from this moment on
his creatures were made free of numbing guilt—
destroying guilt;
made free to live
abundantly.   *Andrew Stallsmith*

Hymn: "It Is Finished, Man of Sorrows," or " 'Tis Finished! The Messiah Dies"

Recitation: **Clippings** (*group of J/T/A*)

From the blotter of the palace police:
   On orders of Pontius Pilate, crucified Dismas, Jesus, and Gesmus.

Clipping from the evening edition of the Jerusalem papers, page 5:
Three men were crucified on Skull Hill this morning. All were pronounced dead at 3:30 P.M. The body of one, Jesus of Nazareth, was claimed by friends. The other two, thieves, were buried in potter's field.

From the editorial page:
Society got rid of three men today. Two men were put to death for living outside the law of the land. One died for living above the laws laid down by our social order in our sacred books. When will men learn that the law is a fence inside which all men must live?

From the science column, evening paper:
The seismograph indicated severe earth tremors at 3:00 P.M. No homes appear damaged, but it has been reported to this office that graves have been damaged in the cemeteries outside Jerusalem.

From a report of the temple custodian:
The great veil before the Holy of Holies tore from top to bottom this afternoon. The curtain is completely ruined. There is no apparent reason for the catastrophe; all members are intact.

Announcement from the death notices:
Jesus, son of Joseph, died by crucifixion this afternoon. Burial took place before sundown in the garden of Joseph of Arimathea. Age 33. He is survived by his mother, Mary, and his brothers and sisters.

From a letter of Paul of Tarsus to the church at Philippi:
"Let this mind be in you, which was also in Christ Jesus: who, being in the form of God, thought it not robbery to be equal with God: but made himself of no reputation, and took upon him the form of a servant, and was made in the likeness of men: and being found in fashion as a man, he humbled himself, and became obedient unto death, even the death of the cross" (Phil. 2:5-8 KJV). *Frederick W. Kemper*

Hymn: "O Love Divine, What Hast Thou Done?"

Recitation: **What Has God Done?** *(T/A)*

> Darkness
> And trembling earth
> A veil is rent
> And thus lays bare
> The very heart of God;
> The seeking, yearning heart of God.
>
> What has God done
> But give himself
> But give himself in agony
> To draw his creatures close;
> To draw me close, in love? *Andrew Stallsmith*

Recitation: **The Cross** *(I/J)*

> It's just an earthly symbol, standing there alone.
> But it shines in all its glory
> like a golden, kingly throne.

18

Yes, it's just a simple token to remember Christ has died.
But the feeling that it gives us
will make us glow inside.   *Jean Conder Soule*

Hymn: "In the Cross of Christ I Glory"
Song: "When Jesus Died upon the Tree"

Recitation: **Jesus, Friend of Sinners** (*T/A*)

> Jesus, friend of sinners,
>   betrayed by a disciple,
>   bound by the temple guard,
>   accused by false witnesses,
>   laughed at by the king,
>   condemned to die,
>   flogged by soldiers,
>   degraded by the governor,
>   crucified,
>   consigned to hell
>   in our stead,
>   thank you.   *Frederick W. Kemper*

Scripture: John 18:1-19, 42

Other materials that can be used are: "Easter Breakthrough," page 22; "No Victory," page 22; "A Prayer," page 23; "If I Can Follow Jesus," page 24.

EASTER

Recitations, Readings, Dramas

You may find the Easter theme best suited to your needs among the following possible combinations.

1. Stand by for a Special Bulletin! *In a pageant embracing all age groups, try for a "media" effect—perhaps with the equipment and atmosphere of a TV studio—and strive to reproduce the quality of immediacy that surrounded the first Easter. Choose from the following as coverage of the Easter Sunday event: "Hear Ye," page 21; "Extra! Extra!" page 21; "Clippings," page 17-18; "The Third Day Came," page 20; "He Lives," page 21; "No Victory," page 22; "The Human Prospect," page 22-23; "Great Ruling Christ," page 23; "Legacy of Lilies," page 24; sections of the plays* Three Views of the Tomb *and* How Could We Have Doubted? *Suggested songs are "Forever, Hallelujah!" and "He Is Risen."*

2. He Is Risen. *For a pageant that concentrates on the excitement inherent both to the initial resurrection discovery and to our renewed discovery that the resurrection promise is constant and continuing, choose from the following: "He Is Risen," page 20; "Laugh and Sing," page 20; "Last Night," page 20; "Hear the Bells," page 21; "No Victory," page 22; "If I Can Follow Jesus," page 24; "Legacy of Lilies," page 24;*

19

and sections from the play How Could We Have Doubted? *Suggested songs are "And That's a Miracle," "Forever, Hallelujah!" "He Is Risen," "Where Has the Little Baby Gone?"*

3. Easter Breakthrough. *In a pageant that crystallizes the unexpectedness of the Easter events—from the shock of unanticipated defeat to unimaginable triumph—and the power generated by this "breakthrough," you may want to include one of the plays:* Three Views of the Tomb, The Denial of Peter, One Mother's Loss, *or portions of* How Could We Have Doubted? *Other materials that could be used are: "Easter Breakthrough," page 22; "The Third Day Came," page 20; "What Can I Say?" page 21; "The Human Prospect," page 22-23; "Great Ruling Christ," page 23; "If I Can Follow Jesus," page 24; "Legacy of Lilies," page 24; "An Easter Lily," page 25. Suggested songs are "Forever, Hallelujah!" "He Is Risen," "Where Has the Little Baby Gone?"*

4. *Begin with the play* Three Views of the Tomb *and then blend in additional viewpoints by using some of the following: "No Victory," page 22; "Great Ruling Christ," page 23; "Legacy of Lilies," page 24; "An Easter Lily," page 25. Suggested songs are "And That's a Miracle," "Forever, Hallelujah!" "He Is Risen."*

5. *Use the play* One's Mother's Loss *to concentrate on the human emotions and perspectives intertwined in the events of Holy Week. Other materials that could be used are: "Last Night," page 20; "The Third Day Came," page 20; "He Lives," page 21; "No Victory," page 22; "The Human Prospect," page 22-23; "A Prayer," page 23; "Legacy of Lilies," page 24. Suggested songs are "Forever, Hallelujah!" "He Is Risen."*

Recitation: **He Is Risen!** (*P/I*)

> He is risen! He is risen!
> He has broken death's dark prison!
> Hallelujah! He is risen!
> He is risen from the dead!

Recitation: **Laugh and Sing** (*P/I*)

> Laugh and sing and dance about—
> Pray and praise and raise a shout—
> Jesus Christ is risen!

Recitation: **Last Night** (*I*)

> Last night, the dismal tomb was sealed.
> Our hearts were filled with sadness.
> But, now! Behold! The stone is rolled
> Away— What perfect gladness!

Recitation: **The Third Day Came** (*P/I*)

> The third day came—a glorious day!
> They saw the stone was rolled away.
> "He lives! He lives!" the women said.
> "Our Lord has risen from the dead!"

Recitation: **Hear Ye** (*P, with a bell, like a town crier*)

> Hear ye! Hear ye! Hear the news!
> Jesus Christ has risen!
> He still lives! He has escaped
> death's dark, dismal prison!

Recitation: **Hear the Bells** (*B*)

> Hear the bells on Easter Day;
> Hear them sing and hear them say:
> "Christ the Lord has risen!"

Recitation: **Extra! Extra!** (*B/P, wears newspaper bag; waves Good News Bible*)

Extra! Extra! Hear the news—Jesus lives today!
Read the Book which tells us so, this happy Easter Day!

Recitation: **What Can I Say?** (*J/T*)

> What can I say that others have not said
> so many times before to honor Christ—
> to magnify his name?
>> Each word—a new and perfect jewel—
>> would not suffice
>> to laud his sacrifice
>> and tell his glory.
> I can but use these old words—new to me—
> words that he most yearns to hear:
> My Lord, I come to thee.   *Andrew Stallsmith*

Recitation: **He Lives** (*J*)

> He lives again!
> Go tell the news
> Go shout it from the highest hills
> Go tell the sin-sick, guilty world
> That he who died for you and me
> Who took our place upon the tree
> Who paid the price to set us free
> That Christ, our Savior
> Lives again!   *Andrew Stallsmith*

Recitation: **An Easter Thank-You** (*group of I*)

> When yellow crocuses appear,
> When skies are bluer and more clear,
> When little buds are bursting out
> And birds return and fly about
>> On feathered wing;

21

When blades of grass are showing green
And April's washed the whole world clean;
When days grow longer—warmer, too,
And all the earth looks fresh and new,
　　　　I want to sing.

When suddenly a soft wind blows
And I can change to lighter clothes,
When I can fly my new red kite
And watch its wiggly tail of white,
　　　　I feel just right!

ALL:　　But I must not forget, you see,
Who plans these wonders, just for me.
So thank you, God, for Easter joy
You bring to every girl and boy
　　　　Each day and night.　　　*Jean Conder Soule*

Recitation: **Easter Breakthrough** (*T/A*)

Through all the loops of pink and blue
The ribbon-packaged Easter eggs,
The cards, the bonnets, and the lilies,
Irrelevance of rabbits
And thankfulness for spring,
A man in simple white approaches,
Walks straight toward us
Pale from loss of blood
But with a firm step;
He's holding out his hand
In recognition,
As though he knew us well
And wished to know us better,
His clear eyes holding promise,
Expecting our response
And offering strength and purpose—
Beginning now.　　　*Andrew T. Roy*

Recitation: **No Victory** (*T/A*)

Every experience of man
says Jesus should not rise from the grave,
　　except Easter—
and all say that man,
being dead is dead,
　　except Christ.　　　*Frederick W. Kemper*

Recitation: **The Human Prospect** (*T/A*)

His eyes were clear; he knew what lay ahead
And yet the prospect did not make him veer.

22

By love constrained, he swept aside his fear
And forced the issue with the blood he shed.

The grave, for three days only, could contain
That life. He rose; he lives. He makes it clear
At what great cost, year after lonely year,
He shapes and makes us ready for God's reign.

Andrew T. Roy

Recitation: **For Easter Joys** (*J*)

Thank you, God, for letting me see
Fronds of green on my willow tree;
Blades of grass and a crocus bud
Peeping out of soft spring mud.
Thank you, God, for letting me hear
A nesting robin's notes of cheer,
A cricket's chirp, the hum of bees
And whisper of wind in new-leafed trees.
It's wonderful, Lord, that my ears and eyes
May witness your seasonal surprise:
The glad rebirth of each living thing
And the wonderful sights and sounds of spring!

Jean Conder Soule

Recitation: **Great Ruling Christ** (*A*)

Great ruling Christ—
The watch was insufficient.
The seal of Pilate was not sacred.
The stone of the door was shattered.
God cannot sleep the sleep of death!
You rose in splendor! Hallelujah!
You reign in majesty! Hosanna!
You rule in equity! Glory to God!

Please, hold my trembling hand.   *Frederick W. Kemper*

Scripture: Mark 16:1-8

Recitation: **A Prayer** (*T/A*)

Lord of the weak in faith;
Christ of the infinite patience;
Lord of the perfect peace—
My Lord and my God,
  Be in our midst;
  Show us the nail holes of our forgiveness
  and the spear wound of our peace;
Calm our frightened hearts;
Quiet our trembling;
Strengthen our faith;
Give us your perfect peace.   *Frederick W. Kemper*

Scripture: John 21:19, 31

Recitation: **If I Can Follow Jesus** (*I/J*)

If I can follow Jesus along the thorny way
And mark the Master's footsteps—I'll come to Easter Day.

I'll see the light of morning, the rising of the sun,
And the darkness will be vanquished
When Good Friday's gloom is done.

So let me watch and listen for the message that I'll hear
When the empty tomb is entered, and there's nothing left to fear.

Yes, I will follow Jesus on the road I know is right,
And at the distant turning,
I'll find the Easter light.
Jean Conder Soule

Scripture: John 20:1-9

Reading: **Legacy of Lilies** (*A*)

Wilda from her hospital bed turned a cheerful smile in my direction. "Go dig up mine. I won't be needing them anymore."

How can she say such things, I thought, wincing. Wilda was dying and she knew it. I did not want to let her go. What she accepted, I rebelled against, for I believed our parting would be final.

We were talking about lilies of the valley. They and lilacs are my favorite flowers, and I had difficulty growing both. This year, for the first time, my ten-year-old lilac bush had produced blossoms, and I had brought Wilda a fragrant armful. My lilies of the valley had remained tiny and green and quickly dried up on their stems.

Like the flowers, my friend was withering away. Almost from day to day, I could see her physically losing ground. Mentally, she was her own dear self, interested in everyone and everything, refusing to turn her attention inward. Her faith was stronger than mine, and I knew this bothered her.

"I can't go dig up your lily-of-the-valley bulbs," I protested. "Next spring you'll probably—"

"Please take them. I want you to have them. Next spring I won't be here."

And she wasn't. She died during the winter. In the spring I watched a lush crop of her lilies of the valley bounce to vigorous life in my garden. I had dug up the bulbs from Wilda's backyard as she had invited me to do, keeping clods of her rich soil around them according to her instructions. How very much they reminded me of her: her always straight back—the flowers' sturdy stems; her strong, honest opinions—the flowers' sweet, sharp fragrance; and the curtailed years of her life—the snowy bells, marching along the stem for too short a time before their fading.

Each spring for the past half dozen years, I have picked Wilda's flowers and put them in the blue ceramic vase she gave me. Wilda comes to life for me again, her resurrection now as assured in my mind as this yearly miracle

24

of renewal, for her spirit—the essence of her personality—cannot die. She lived and will live again. Her flowers say it—spring after spring.

All the seemingly worthwhile things she owned were left for her relatives, as they should have been. She left me a small vase she had made herself, and some lily-of-the-valley bulbs. I think my friend knew exactly what she was doing when she gave them to me. *Marjorie Murch Stanley*

Reading: **An Easter Lily** (*J/T*)

It is Easter Sunday; our little church has just been painted. All week I watched the painters cover the church with long sweeps of white. "You wanna help, boy?" they asked me. So I helped paint around the two front windows. The painters laughed and patted my head, saying I did a good job. It is a fine thing to paint a church the color of snow.

The grass in front is newly mowed. At the bottom of the churchyard where the ground slopes down and the stones rise like teeth, the grass is long and green. The wind sings there. The caretaker says the ground is wet and the uncut grass drinks up the moisture. I like the quietness of the place. I like the grave of the Civil War soldier. John Whitacre, killed by a cannonball, is on the stone. Here I pretend that I'm the drummer boy at Shiloh. I can see the blue and gray coats fall like leaves in a wild wind. Then the far-off lonely whistle of the incoming train brings me back.

This morning, each of us in the children's choir carried a lily down the aisle. It is an Easter tradition at our church. Later, I took mine to my mother's grave. I have a habit of talking to her when no one else is around. "Mother," I said, settling down in the sweet grass, "I sang in the choir today— I was a good boy this Easter. I emptied my pockets of frogs and stones and took a bath and combed my hair. I wanted you to be proud of me.

"Mother, I knew you were there, this morning. You were sitting in the empty pew. The sun shone, and I saw the gold of your hair. When church was over, I sat there for awhile. It was soft and warm, as though your arms were holding me.

"I know God came to the service, too. For outside the new buds trembled on the trees, and the songbirds stopped singing for a moment.

"Easter is sad without you, Mother. I know you are somewhere above me. I like to think that you help God paint the rainbows and that you fluff up the clouds each day.

"All I can give you this Easter is the lily which was given to me. I hear the bells chiming and I can see the ribbon of smoke from the two o'clock train. I must go, or I'll be late for dinner.

"Mother, I'll be back in June, when the roses bloom." *Elaine Delp*

Three Views of the Tomb

(an Easter drama for teens and adults)

Characters: Lucius, Octavius, Joseph, Nicodemus, Mary
Setting: *Front of sanctuary where two Roman soldiers, Lucius and Octavius, begin to move slowly toward the back as they speak.*

25

LUCIUS:	I have the strangest feeling tonight.
OCTAVIUS:	It's boredom. Frustration. Anger—given this stupid graveside duty, where the only action is lizards darting from stone to cactus.
LUCIUS:	No. It's more than that. I feel— (*Shivers*)
OCTAVIUS:	(*Laughing*) Not frightened, surely! You've seen enough of death not to be shaken by one more dead Jew! He's safe enough, shut in behind that rock. I helped move it there, remember? And Jupiter himself would need a thunderbolt or two to budge it!
LUCIUS:	Please. Don't joke.
OCTAVIUS:	Jupiter won't mind. We go a long way back, we two.
LUCIUS:	But there are—other gods.
OCTAVIUS:	(*Comfortably*) Ah, yes! A stableful, in fact! Rolling their casual and prophetic dice, deciding that we two pace here tonight yawning while the others carouse in town.
LUCIUS:	I meant—
OCTAVIUS:	(*Unbelieving*) Not the Hebrew God, you mean! Don't waste a thought for him! All that bowing and scraping those fools do—that chanting to All-Powerful! All-Powerful, indeed! Who *is* it who wields the power here, I ask! The legions of Rome, is who—and those dogs know it. They scuttle like frightened rats when armor rattles—their god forgotten.
LUCIUS:	They say—that that's his Son— (*Gestures back*)
OCTAVIUS:	(*Laughing*) Yes, so some say. Which proves my point, I'd think. (*Claps younger man on back*) Not too impressive, would you say, dying that way? Where was this Hebrew god while rabble crucified his son? Hmmmm? (*More briskly*) Come, now! Brace up! This is deadly dull duty we've drawn, but moping won't improve it. Morning will dawn and shame these youthful tremors. The rock will still rest firmly in its place, and night's shadows—and its sounds—will melt in sunlight. Come, now! I know a certain cure for weakened knees and tight-strung nerves. Have you yet heard the joke about—
	They are at the back, now. Joseph of Arimathea *and* Nicodemus *appear and reach front center as soldiers speak last line.* Joseph's *first words overlap the last line* Octavius *speaks.*
JOSEPH:	A garden seems the fitting place for him. (*Pause*) Especially *this* garden, where I have walked for hours at a time, seeking to pull the peacefulness of this quiet place into my

seething brain, wondering—more perhaps than anything else—about the things he said, those promises he made—promises evil men have stamped into the dust, never to rise again—*perhaps*— (*Pause, as he paces*) Gardens have always seemed such symbols to me. Symbols of life—the abundant life that he said we should live. But, more than that—symbols of death, close followed by rebirth.

NICODEMUS: You must be born again, he told me, when I stole to him one night, my mind a maelstrom of conflicting issues, warring against itself. Such an impossibility—to enter the safety of the womb once more, once more to be thrust out and pushed, unready, toward the hostile world. (*More quietly*) Such an unhappy thought, to face it all again—

JOSEPH: Yet life with him, through him, was something beautiful. Secure. Pulsing with promise, warm with love. (*Spoken with agony*) How shall we ever live without him—having known him once? You must be born again, he said—and showed us how! (*Pause*) Then how can we deny him now with this dread deadness of our spirits?

NICODEMUS: (*Shrugging*) How can we do otherwise? Evil has triumphed as we thought it never might again. Shadows of evil stalk the streets, ride the night breezes, cackling their hatreds toward the throne of God. We tasted sweetness through his word. Is it not natural that the bitterness we know should be thrice bitter for the sweetness briefly tasted?

JOSEPH: Natural—perhaps. But there was nothing natural in these recent months. Unnatural peace—unnatural hope—unnatural joy—unnatural lives erupting from cocoons of ancient hopelessness. (*Pause*) How can we let it go?

NICODEMUS: Again, can we do otherwise? (*Striding about*) We have done all we might, just now. You have provided him this sepulchre, set in a fragrant garden. And I have furnished spices for anointing— (*Breaks off, stricken*) O God! O God! Did you not hear us when we prayed our joyous prayers of bright rebirth? Could you not bend from tyrant God to that bright, loving Father he portrayed? Where is your mercy now? Your sweet forgiveness? No myrrh or spikenard can relieve the stench of all our dying dreams.

JOSEPH: My friend, control your grief. If God were as you paint him, he would strike you dead.

NICODEMUS: If he were what we thought him, as we listened—then Christ would not be dead.

JOSEPH: (*Gently*) Walk quietly here, my friend. Allow this rising sun, these flowering herbs, to bring you peace.

27

NICODEMUS: There is no peace for me unless I hear his voice again and read compassion in his eyes.

They exit. Soft music is heard. The front of the sanctuary is empty at this time, but as the last strains die away, Mary *runs from the back of the church. Wild-eyed, glowing, she moves about as she speaks. She gestures excitedly, sometimes mingles with the congregation, and addresses the people directly.*

MARY: I have seen him! He has spoken to me! He lives! He lives! And we live, too! Watching, we died with him! Walking and talking, we were corpses—*worse* than dead, because the pain remained. The pain—that dreadful, searing pain— But now! He lives! And in my rotting soul, new life has sprung—as here—see here? (*Stooping, as though picking up soil*) New shoots push through the loam. (*Moving forward into the congregation, speaking softly*) All that he said is true. *Is true!* As he lives, so do I! And so can everyone! Feel in your heart the stirrings of that love, that promise of eternal blooming! Oh, what a joyous ringing in these stones! What singing surges through my veins! He lives! *He lives! He lives!* No sweeter words than these—for all eternity!

One Mother's Loss

(a play for teens and adults)
by Frances C. Pratt

Characters: Mother of Jesus, Mary Magdalene, John, narrator, voices in crowd, centurion, Jesus' voice, angel
Setting: *Although the scene is set in Bible times, the speech and emotions are those of today. The play opens with soft music.*

Scene 1: Mary, *the mother of Jesus, and* Magdalene *are in the kitchen, talking.*

MOTHER: You can't be *serious*, Mary Magdalene!

MAGDALENE: But I tell you, Mary, there's going to be trouble! Just today at the well the women were talking. They said the Sanhedrin won't tolerate any more nonsense from Jesus! (*Voice quivers*) I'm not trying to frighten you, Mary, but somewhere, inside, I feel sure this isn't just gossip! (*Paces*) How can you sit there, so calm, so *unfeeling!*

MOTHER: (*Looking up, face troubled*) Magdalene!

MAGDALENE: I'm sorry. That was unfair. But I'm so upset! Mark my words, no good can come of this!

MOTHER: (*Stirring kettle*) But, my dear, how can you or I know what is "good"? Who knows God's plans? What we must remem-

28

ber is that Jesus is not only my son; he's God's. And surely God knows what is happening. (*Doesn't sound quite sure*) Do you think it hurts any less because I know Jesus was only loaned to Joseph and me? Oh, Magdalene (*Drops face in hands*) I'm afraid this burden is too great.

Mary Magdalene *stoops and puts her arms around her. Sound of running footsteps outside is heard.* John, *very much upset, enters.*

JOHN: Mary! They've done it! The chief priests and elders came while we were on Mount Olive and took Jesus! You should have seen that Judas! (*With contempt*) How sickening sweet he was, coming up and kissing Jesus, then turning him over to the mob! (*Pauses to catch breath*) Some of us grabbed up clubs and Peter even took his sword and started swinging. He cut off the ear of one of the fellows.

The two women *wait in frozen fear.*

MAGDALENE: Then?

JOHN: Then, you might know. Jesus put his ear back on and it quit bleeding, just like that! (*Snaps fingers*)

MOTHER: (*Nodding*) Yes, that's just what Jesus would do. (*Fearfully*) But where is my son now, John?

JOHN: They took him to the house of the chief priest. I saw him go in, then I ran here to tell you.

MOTHER: (*Starting to rise*) Then I must go and be with him.

JOHN: (*Pressing back against door*) No! There's nothing you can do. And he'd feel worse to have you see him this way.

MOTHER: *What* way?

JOHN: (*Stammering*) Why—tied up, naturally. (*Takes deep breath*) No, Mary, you stay right here. But I'll be back and bring word just as soon as I hear something. (*Turns toward door*) Take care of her, Magdalene.

John *leaves.* Magdalene *puts kettle on to heat.*

MAGDALENE: I'll make some tea, Mary. It's going to be a long night. (*Light fades slowly, to darkness*)

NARRATOR: It was, indeed, a long night. In the morning, it was John who brought word that Jesus had appeared before Pilate, who had, in turn, sent him to Herod who had returned him to Pilate. (*Light slowly rises, same scene*)

JOHN: He still tried to let him go— (*Voice drops*)

MAGDALENE: Well—*couldn't* he?

JOHN: No. No, he couldn't. That entire, cursed crowd kept yelling and crying for Jesus' blood!

29

MOTHER:	(*Barely audible*) So?
JOHN:	(*Voice choked*) And so—they've taken him to Golgotha.
MOTHER:	(*Leaving stool, clutches John about the legs*) Golgotha! That's where they—
JOHN:	(*Gently taking her face in his hands*) Yes. Yes, Mary. They've crucified him.
MOTHER:	(*Clinging to him, her hands twisted in his cloak, her face upturned*) I *must* go, John.

John *starts to refuse, then relents. At last, he stoops and helps her to her feet. Then, supported between* John *and* Mary Magdalene, Mary *begins the long, painful walk to Golgotha. The three may exit by the sanctuary aisle and return as the* narrator *speaks.*

NARRATOR:	The streets of the city were empty. They passed no one as they stumbled up the hill. Everyone had gone to the crucifixion. At last they reached the fringes of the crowd. Mary kept her eyes lowered, unable to look at the people who were seated on the ground, eating lunches with a holiday air. As they pushed through the standing throngs, every now and then someone would recognize them.
VOICE 1:	There's one of them, now!
2:	And his mother!
3:	And that harlot who was always chasing him!
4:	She's got a nerve!

Scene 2: Golgotha. The shadows of three crosses are cast upon a sheet background. Jesus is heard but not seen.

NARRATOR:	At last they reached a small clearing near the foot of the cross. Mary looked up at the tall young man, her eyes searching his face which was shadowed, and hung upon his breast. Her gaze shifted to the hands, where the metal spikes had been pounded, and to his feet. With horrible fascination, she watched the slow, dark drip of his blood stain the wood below.
MOTHER:	(*Her knees buckle; John catches her*) Jesus! Oh, Son! *My little boy!*
JESUS' VOICE:	Mother! You shouldn't have come. (*Pause*) Please, Mother, don't cry. It's going to be all right. (*Voice grows weaker, then strengthens again*) John! After I'm gone, Mother will need someone. I'd like you to take care of her. Will you promise?
JOHN:	You know I will.
VOICE:	(*A few moments later, crying out*) It is finished!

30

MOTHER:	He's gone! Oh, bless him, he's gone!
NARRATOR:	Just then there was a sudden darkening of the sky, a sound of thunder, coming closer. The sun, so unbearably hot, disappeared, and the wind arose. (*Drums, swelling*) The earth quivered underfoot. Suddenly, as the crowd watched in open-mouthed horror, a bolt of lightning (*Light and sound*) hurtled from the sky, straight toward the temple. Stones were thrown afar, and the veil of the temple was torn in two. (*Pause*) The crowd, now, was quiet. Gone was the merrymaking. Frightened eyes stared from stark faces. Here and there were whispers.
CENTURION:	(*Removing helmet, falling to knees*) Surely this was the Son of God! Heaven help us now!
NARRATOR:	But Mary was looking up at Jesus, not seeing a mangled body sagging on a torture stake, but remembering the bright figure of an angel who had come to her before Jesus was born. She remembered her fright of this heavenly being, and then—the worst fear of all—he had told her she would bear the Son of God and bring him up to young manhood. Her face burned again with the shame she had felt at what people were going to say, since everyone knew she and Joseph had not yet taken their final vows. But when the child had been born—in that unlikely barn in Bethlehem—and she had seen him—how little it had mattered what anyone thought or said.
	As he had grown, he used to come and talk with her while she baked. It was those times she remembered especially, for they had shared each other's thoughts, and she had grown to wonder at the mind of her son. He used to warn her that he wouldn't be with her too long, but that she shouldn't fear. God, his Father, had it all figured out and it would be all right—even as he had just now said! She remembered with a pang of fresh sorrow how she had clung to him and argued and fussed and tried to get him to change his mind, but he had looked at her with such a peculiar expression that she had finally kept quiet.
MOTHER:	He's done nothing to deserve this! It's not fair! *It's just not fair!* (*Voice rises wildly*)
	A soldier *with a drawn sword approaches* Jesus. John *turns* Mary *away.*
JOHN:	Come. There's nothing more we can do here. Let's take her home, Magdalene.
NARRATOR:	This time, Mary made no protest and let them lead her back down the stony path toward an empty house.
	They exit.

31

Scene 3:   Late on the Sabbath in the kitchen.

NARRATOR: Mary awoke from sorrow-drugged sleep to find that it was afternoon on a dark and sunless Sabbath. When Mary Magdalene saw her stir, she arose from a stool and offered her a cup of tea.

Neither woman speaks; Mary *obediently sips tea.*

MOTHER: (*At last, her voice dull*) Where are the others?

MAGDALENE: Scattered. In hiding, mostly.

MOTHER: And John?

MAGDALENE: I don't know. He left last night after bringing you home. He said he would return when he had news. (*Takes empty cup from Mary*) Until then, try to rest, won't you?

MOTHER: Listen! Someone's coming! (*Brightens, then sags back*) I thought for a minute they were Jesus' steps. I can't seem to remember he won't be coming back anymore.

MAGDALENE: *Don't,* Mary! Don't let yourself think that way! (*Swings toward the door at stealthy sound, whispering*) But someone *is* coming.

John *slips in, uncovering hood from his face.*

MAGDALENE: (*Relieved*) John! What's the news?

JOHN: The friends are in hiding, as you can guess. But I did hear one piece of news I thought you'd like to know. Joseph from Arimathea, who's a respected member of the Council, went to Pilate and asked if he could bury Jesus. Imagine! It makes the rest of us look like cowards. Anyway, Pilate said he could, so he laid Jesus in a cave. It has a great stone in front of the opening, though. I heard Pilate had set a guard to keep anyone from going near. I guess he's afraid we'll steal the body and pretend he arose—you know, like he once said.

MAGDALENE: (*Hopefully*) You— You don't think he *might*?

JOHN: (*Sighing*) I don't know. Honestly. I saw Jesus work miracles and I know they were real. I could have believed anything, then. But now—I mean—if you or I had died, I think Jesus could have raised us back to life. But he's the one who's dead! Who's going to raise *him*? (*All are silent, hopeless*) Well, I'd better go, but if you need me, send word. I'll be at Simon's on the street of the silversmiths in an upstairs room. If I hear anything more, I'll try to let you know. (*Slips out quietly. Light fades to darkness*)

Scene 4:   Before dawn, on the road to the tomb. Mary *hurries, obviously trying to avoid notice.*

MAGDALENE: (*Catching up to her*) Where are you going?

32

MOTHER:	Ssssh! I'm going to the tomb.
MAGDALENE:	Do you dare? I mean, with the soldiers— What are you carrying?
MOTHER:	This? Oh, just spices. I thought maybe I could talk them into letting me in—you know, being his mother.
MAGDALENE:	I'll never understand you. One minute you sit back and let everyone trample all over you. The next, all Caesar's soldiers can't keep you away. (*Pause*) Well, I expect I'll have to go with you.
MOTHER:	Nonsense. Go home.
MAGDALENE:	No. I'm coming with you.
MOTHER:	Well, then, do be quiet.
	Sounds of running feet, of clanking swords, gasping men. A centurion *rushes past them.*
MAGDALENE:	(*Looking after him in awe*) I wonder what's the matter.
MOTHER:	He looked frightened.
MAGDALENE:	He was! He really was!
MOTHER:	Well, never mind him. Let's go on. (*Light brightens*)
MAGDALENE:	(*Suddenly pointing, crying out*) Look!
	They have reached the tomb. Before them stands an angel, *dressed in white. He smiles; both* women *fall to their knees, frightened, but curious.*
ANGEL:	Mary. Greetings from your son, Jesus, the Christ!
MOTHER:	Why—why, we've met before. You came long ago to tell me of his birth!
ANGEL:	That's true. And now I am here to tell you that he is no longer among the dead. He arose not long ago and asked me to tell you when you came that he has arisen—is living right now—and will see you later!
MOTHER:	(*With wild joy*) Jesus! He's alive! Oh, Magdalene, he's alive! (*Throws her arms around Mary Magdalene, embracing her, then turns back to the angel*) Truly? He really is?
ANGEL:	(*Smiling gently*) He really is. And he said for you not to worry; everything will be all right.
MAGDALENE:	Oh, Mary! Let's go tell John and the others! Won't they be surprised? (*Tugs on Mary's arm*)
MOTHER:	(*Standing straight, radiant*) Not yet, Magdalene. You go on, if you like. I want to stay here for a few moments—alone.
	Mary Magdalene *exits, running.* Mary *sinks onto a stump—a low stool may be used—raises her head and looks at the angel.*
MOTHER:	But I still don't see—I don't understand! If he was going to rise from the dead, why did he die at all?

ANGEL: Humans can't expect to understand the ways of God, but I can tell you this: God has always required a blood sacrifice for sin. Now Jesus has become that sacrifice for sin, once and for all, for everybody! Not only that, your son has made death nothing more than passing from this life to another! In the ages to come, when he sets up his kingdom and becomes the promised king, everyone will praise his name!

MOTHER: *(Nodding, bowing head)* You're right. It's too much for me to understand. But this much I know— How small is my loss compared to the world's gain. Hallelujah!

Music: "Hallelujah Chorus"

How Could We Have Doubted?

(a play with music)

Characters: Four or six speakers (*I/J*), three women, angel

Four speakers *in biblical costume enter, walking slowly, dejectedly.*

SPEAKER 1: I never really thought he'd go away.

2: I always really thought he'd stay.

3: The things he said—the things he did—

4: Remember how he made a blind man see?
Remember all the things he said to me?

ALL: *How could he die?*

SPEAKER 1: Or—dying—shouldn't he have known?

2: How was it that he talked about his throne?

3: I loved him, but—I somehow feel betrayed.
I keep remembering the promises he made—
that he'd be with us, everywhere we walked;
that he would give us all the words we needed as we talked—
at least I *thought* he promised that—did you?
I thought that all the things he said—were true.

ALL: We thought that he had come to be a king,
to wear a crown and robe, as all kings do.
We thought that he had come to change an evil world—
to take the old and broken, to make the ragged new.
That's what we thought. *(Pause)*
We thought that he had come to make the dingy bright,
to draw a brilliant day from darkest night—
to heal the sick and lame, to make the weary sing,
to make the ugly beautiful—to be our king.
That's what we thought.
(Sadly, slowly) But he is dead, instead,
and all our hopes died with him.

34

SPEAKER 3:	I—feel—betrayed. And yet—I wonder—
ALL:	Why should we be sad and dreary? Why should we be wan and weary—walking with our dragging footsteps heavy in the sand? Didn't he—while he was with us—promise that he'd always lead us—that he'd lead us by his loving hand? Shouldn't we, then, though he's taken, act more cherished than forsaken? Shouldn't we remember how it was when he was here? Can't we just ignore his dying? Can't we now survive this sighing? Can't we simply close our eyes, and can't we just pretend he's with us still? *(Pause)*

Song: "How Ever Many Days"

After song, speakers *nod solemnly, sigh, and exit. Pause.* Three women, *carrying spices, enter at back of church. They walk slowly, at first, but react to words of the song as they move slowly down the aisle. They pantomime stooping to enter the tomb, then they express their amazement.*

WOMEN:	*(Together)* Jesus Christ is risen! That's what the angel said! Jesus Christ, the Son of God, is risen from the dead! *They exit quickly down the aisle.*
ANGEL:	The empty cross is just a part of Easter's story—for Christ was taken from the cross by *human* hands, and human tears were flowing, and human hearts were weeping as he was carried from the cross into the tomb where there was room—a chill and chiseled room—a room designed for death. *(Pause)* But *Christ* was not designed for death—nor death for him. No, death had not the strength to keep him still; and death had not a coldness deep enough that it could chill his warmth—his love—his loving Spirit. Death tried to hold him, but he wrenched away, and still he lives today! *(Exits)* *The* four speakers *reenter and stand. From the back of the church, the* women *run to them.*
WOMAN 1:	*(Excitedly)* He *lives!*
SPEAKER 2:	*Who* lives?
WOMAN 2:	*He* lives!
SPEAKER 3:	*(Amazed) He lives?*
WOMAN 3:	He lives! We saw! We know! The angels told us there that it was so!

Song: "And That's a Miracle!" *(all)*

SPEAKER 1:	He lives!
SPEAKERS 1/2:	He lives!
	Continue to add one more person each time as the words are spoken until all are saying it together, building to a joyful crescendo.

SPEAKER 1:   I knew that he would never go away!

2:   I always really knew he'd stay.

3:   The things he said—the things he did—

4:   Remember how he made a blind man see?
Remember all the things he said to me?

Hymn: "Christ the Lord Is Risen Today!"

SPEAKER 4 or 5: Yes, Jesus lives today. He lives in you and me.
He lives in all we say and all we do.
He lives each time we speak in love;
he lives each time we smile;
He lives each time we speak his name,
each time we tell his story;
each time we raise our hearts in prayer,
or sing his glory.
He lives. He lives. He *lives!*

SPEAKER 1 or 6: Yes, Jesus lives today. I see him everywhere.
I feel him in the breeze that stirs the air.
I see him in the wonders of spring's returning green.
No matter where I turn, his love is seen.
I hear him in the songs of birds; I hear him in the wind;
I touch him when I touch another's hand.
I know that he is with me—around me and within.
When I invited him, he took the place of sin—
and now he lives in me. He lives. He lives. He *lives!*

Song: Choose one of those in the back of this book.

Other materials that can be used with this play are: "Easter Breakthrough," page 22; "No Victory," page 22; "Great Ruling Christ," page 23; "If I Can Follow Jesus," page 24; "Legacy of Lilies," page 24.

HOLY WEEK
General Programs

The following two exercises cover Holy Week and can be presented at any time during the week. Or they can be used in segments, at a number of services. Colored placards may be used with the choral reading. They can be cut into symbolic shapes or appropriate symbols can be drawn boldly on rectangular-shaped cards. Consider using fluorescent colors and black light for a highly dramatic effect.

Choral Reading: **Colors of Holy Week** (*All ages form small groups across stage or chancel and hold cards appropriate for their readings. Groups are identified by age level and number.*)

GROUP 1 (*I*):	Yellow of sunlight—hot in the sky— Warming the crowd as the Savior rides by.
GROUP 2 (*I*):	Green of the branches waving before him— Proving that children respect and adore him.
GROUP 3 (*I/J*):	White of the donkey—white of the dove— White of the light which exemplifies love.
GROUP 4 (*I*):	Pink flush of cheeks proves excitement—belief— Hosanna! The Savior brings peace and relief! *pause and shift of mood*
ALL:	Green touch of envy—dark fingers of greed— Purple enrages with violent speed; Secrets expanding in shadowy dark— Plans taking form to sputter and spark— Soft laughter of evil; hands shaken in spite; such plans must be laid in the deepest of night— The night of the spirit—night of lost souls— where God is shut out; where Satan controls. *pause*
GROUP 5 (*J*):	Blue of Gethsemane's lengthening night. Blue, cool and deep, the beginnings of fright.
6 (*J*):	Purple of royalty—pompous and cruel— grasping and vicious—determined to rule.
5 (*J*):	Black of betrayal, disguised as a friend. Black of a night which seems never to end.
6 (*J*):	Orange of the flames—ruddy, flaring and bright— set in a brazier, a glow in the night.
5 (*J*):	Dark blush of anguish; red tinge of shame. Three times—as the cock crows—Peter bows in self-blame.
7 (*J/T*):	Dark, twisted judgment; a wife's dream of warning. No basin, no water, can ease Pilate's gray morning. *pause*
8 (*T*):	Brown of the thorns in Christ's cruel, mocking crown; brown of the cross which weighted him down; brown of Golgotha—the long, dusty way— and the thoughts of the people who mourned him that day.
5 (*J*):	Red of the blood from hands, feet, head, and side— Red—and our Savior— (*pause*) crucified. *pause*
3 (*I/J*):	Black of two nights—black of the tomb black of depression, of anguish and gloom. *slight pause; then quickly together as chorus*

ALL: And then—*brilliant—exploding*—vivid with power—
        piercing—expanding—igniting the hour—
        the reversal of death, the quiet rending of stone,
        the renewal of tissue and muscle and bone—
        the red-gold of dawning, soft surging of praise—
        and the white light of God introduces the days
        when death cannot conquer, when love governs within—
        and the strong, risen Christ can obliterate sin!

        trumpet fanfare, followed by triumphant hymn

During the recitation of the following poem, show slides of Christian art that illustrates the life of Christ, spotlight live scenes in tableau, or show art produced by group. Consider song "Where Has the Little Baby Gone?" as an appropriate parallel.

Poem: **Angels** (*T/A, six speakers*)

1: Decades before, they'd come to earth   *Scene: Nativity*
    to celebrate a Savior's birth—
    angels who caroled songs of joy,
    directing shepherds to a boy
    who welded, in his tiny length,
    man's weakness with God's cosmic strength.

2: And as—with his maturing eyes—   *Scene: Childhood*
    He watched the foolish and the wise—   *— carpenter shop*
    interpreting his world's events
    with quick and kind intelligence—   *Scene: In temple*
    learning to craft—skillful and sure—
    questions of depth—and furniture—
    perhaps the angels smiled to see
    fulfillment of rich prophecy.

3: While Satan promised—tempting him—   *Scene: Temptation*
    angels would satisfy his whim,
    the Savior—grown into a man—
    continued work that God began,   *Scene: Healing*
    and never summoned from the air
    the unseen angels, waiting there.
    Instead, with gentle, healing art,   *Scene: Teaching*
    He ministered to sinful hearts.

4: Did angels yearn to intercede,   *Scene: Bearing*
    to cancel cruelty and greed,   *cross*
    to neutralize an evil pride   *Scene: Crucifixion*
    that saw a Savior crucified?
    Surely, it would have brought relief
    to voice their anger and their grief.

5: And yet—angelic silence held,   *Scene: Removal*
    and only human anguish welled   *from cross*
    to swell quiet choruses and cries,
    imploring mercy from the skies.

38

6: Two days—two endless days, the tomb—
prepared and filled—increased the gloom
his followers endured with pain.
The third day—heaven ruled again.
No choir of angels swarmed the skies—
nor was their power exercised—
but—contemplatively—one said,
"Why seek ye him—among the dead?"

Scene: Sealed tomb

Scene: Women to tomb

Scene: Empty tomb

Scene: Angels in tomb

MUSIC NOTES

The primary purpose of Christian music is that it be an effective vehicle for the text. Lovely melodies and catchy rhythms draw us to certain songs, but they should never detract from or overshadow the message.

Although some of the music in this anthology is suitable for adult choirs, most of the songs will be sung by children. Care has been taken to use melodies that are easy to sing and memorize. The accompaniment is designed for the second- or third-year piano student to play, thus increasing the participation of children in their own programs. Chord symbols are given so that the more capable musician can improvise and give greater support to the singers, when needed.

The dynamics have been omitted so that the director can be free to treat the music creatively. Occasional, suggested harmonies have been given for the more capable choirs. However, it is far better to emphasize learning the words, melodies, and rhythms correctly than it is to be concerned with too much choral interpretation or harmony when those efforts would detract from the performance of the music. In most cases, the mood of the song is its own dynamic guide. Take care to keep tempos moving and ritardandos at a minimum.

When young or inexperienced choirs are singing canons, it is a good idea to have everyone sing the entire song through once to establish pitch and momentum. Then, without breaking the tempo, have the first group begin. When the number of repetitions has been established, have each group repeat the final phrase until the choir is in unison again. This method is especially effective when the choir is small and the ending group would sound weak in comparison to the whole choir. Incidentally, singing canons is an effective way to begin teaching part singing to young voices.

Barbara Seaborn

BEGINNERS
    Colors of Holy Week (*some parts*), 36
    Extra! Extra! 21
    Foot Washers, 15
    Hear the Bells, 21
    This Palm Branch I Hold, 6
Song:
    "When Jesus Died upon the Tree," 43

PRIMARIES
    Colors of Holy Week (*some parts*), 36
    Extra! Extra! 21
    Foot Washers, 15
    Hear Ye, 21
    He Is Risen, 20
    Laugh and Sing, 20
    See Him Riding, 5
    The Third Day Came, 20
Songs:
    "Come, Praise and Sing Hosanna!" 44
    "He Is Risen" (*canon in four parts*), 44
    "How Ever Many Days," 48
    "When Jesus Died upon the Tree," 43

INTERMEDIATES
    Colors of Holy Week (*some parts*), 36
    The Cross, 18
    An Easter Thank-You, 21
    Foot Washers, 15
    For Palm Sunday, 5
    He Is Risen, 20
    How Could We Have Doubted? (*play*), 34
    Hurry, Hurry! 4
    If I Can Follow Jesus, 24
    I've Looked and Looked and Looked, 5
    Last Night, 20
    Laugh and Sing, 20
    The Parade of Palms, 4, 7
    The Third Day Came, 20
Songs:
    "And That's a Miracle," 41
    "Come, Praise and Sing Hosanna!" 44
    "He Is Risen" (*canon in four parts*), 44
    "How Ever Many Days," 48
    "When Jesus Died upon the Tree," 43
    "Where Has the Little Baby Gone?" 46

JUNIORS
    Acronym, 7
    Clippings, 17-18
    Colors of Holy Week, 36
    The Cross, 18
    An Easter Lily, 25
    Foot Washers, 15
    For Easter Joys, 23
    Golgotha, 16
    He Lives, 21
    How Could We Have Doubted? (*play*), 34
    Hurry, Hurry! 4
    I Do Not Know, 16
    If I Can Follow Jesus, 24
    What Can I Say? 21
Songs:
    "And That's a Miracle," 41
    "Bitter," 47
    "Come, Praise and Sing Hosanna!" 44
    "Forever, Hallelujah!" 43
    "He Is Risen" (*canon in two parts*), 45
    "He Is Risen" (*canon in four parts*), 44
    "Hosanna" (*canon in four parts*), 45
    "How Ever Many Days," 48
    "I Saw a King Today," 42
    "Lord, Why Me?" 48
    "Where Has the Little Baby Gone?" 46

TEENS
    Angels, 38
    Clippings, 17-18
    Colors of Holy Week, 36
    The Denial of Peter (*play*), 10
    Easter Breakthrough, 22
    An Easter Lily, 25
    Ecce Homo, 16
    Finished, 17
    Foot Washers, 15
    Golgotha, 16
    The Human Prospect, 22
    I Do Not Know, 16
    I, Judas, Betrayer of a Friend (*monologue*), 8
    Jesus, Friend of Sinners, 19
    Lifted Up, 17
    No Victory, 22
    One Mother's Loss (*play*), 28
    Palm Sunday Tribute, 6
    A Prayer, 23
    Question, 16
    Three Views of the Tomb (*play*), 25
    Two Points, 6
    What Can I Say? 21
    What Has God Done? 18
Songs:
    "And That's a Miracle," 41
    "Bitter," 47
    "Forever, Hallelujah!" 43
    "He Is Risen" (*canon in two parts*), 45
    "Hosanna" (*canon in four parts*), 45
    "I Saw a King Today," 42
    "Lord, Why Me?" 48
    "Where Has the Little Baby Gone?" 46

ADULTS
    Angels, 38
    Clippings, 17-18
    Colors of Holy Week, 36
    The Denial of Peter (*play*), 10
    Easter Breakthrough, 22
    Ecce Homo, 16
    Finished, 17
    Foot Washers, 15
    Golgotha, 16
    Great Ruling Christ, 23
    The Human Prospect, 22
    I, Judas, Betrayer of a Friend (*monologue*), 8
    Jesus, Friend of Sinners, 19
    Legacy of Lilies, 24
    Lifted Up, 17
    No Victory, 22
    One Mother's Loss (*play*), 28
    Palm Sunday Tribute, 6
    A Prayer, 23
    Question, 16
    Three Views of the Tomb (*play*), 25
    Two Points, 6
    What Has God Done? 18
Songs:
    "Hosanna" (*canon in four parts*), 45
    "Lord, Why Me?" 48

40

AND THAT'S A MIRACLE

Arr. by Barbara Seaborn

Words and music by
Evelyn Minshull

1. He lives, he lives, he lives! And that's a mir - a -
2. He lives, he lives, he lives! And that's a mir - a -

cle, a mir - a - cle that swells with - in my soul.
cle, a mir - a - cle that warms my heart and mind.

A mir - a - cle as grand; a mir - a - cle as
A mir - a - cle I feel; a mir - a - cle as

great as when he touched and made the lep - ers whole.
real as when he healed the sick, the lame, and blind.

I SAW A KING TODAY

J. E. Laird

I saw a King to-day come rid - ing through our town.
I was quite sur - prised to hear he was a king.

The peo - ple stopped and stared, some smiled and some frowned.
He did - n't wear a crown of gold, pur-ple robes or a sig-net ring.

Teach - er said he was a king as she raised her hands up high.

Aa - ron said he was a king by the spar - kle in his eye.

I knew he was a king when he looked at me and smiled.

But some - thing in his eyes made me cry.

The King was on a colt as he trav - eled through our town.

I was sure he was a king, though Mom - my said he was

just a clown.

FOREVER, HALLELUJAH!

Words and music by
Barbara Seaborn

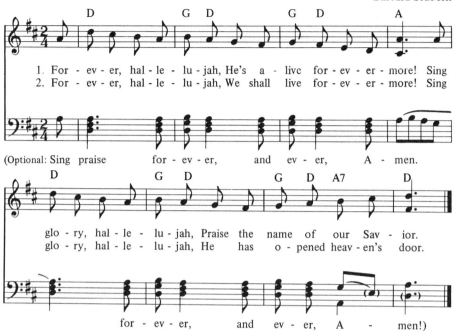

1. For - ev - er, hal - le - lu - jah, He's a - live for - ev - er - more! Sing
2. For - ev - er, hal - le - lu - jah, We shall live for - ev - er - more! Sing

(Optional: Sing praise for - ev - er, and ev - er, A - men.

glo - ry, hal - le - lu - jah, Praise the name of our Sav - ior.
glo - ry, hal - le - lu - jah, He has o - pened heav - en's door.

for - ev - er, and ev - er, A - men!)

Note: The familiar motif from Handel's "Hallelujah Chorus" is given in the bass and provides an effective optional counter melody when sung by male voices. The melody is in the upper notes except where indicated by parentheses.

WHEN JESUS DIED UPON THE TREE

Words and music by
Barbara Seaborn

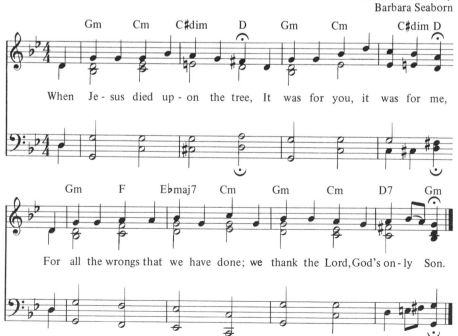

When Je - sus died up - on the tree, It was for you, it was for me,

For all the wrongs that we have done; we thank the Lord, God's on - ly Son.

43

COME, PRAISE AND SING HOSANNA!

Arr. by Barbara Seaborn

Words and music by
Evelyn Minshull

Come, claim my King as your King, too, Come, praise and sing ho - san - na! Come
fol - low him in all you do, Come, praise and sing ho - san - na! Lay

palm leaves down be - fore him; Come wor - ship and a - dore him. Come,

know my Lord as your Lord, too. Come praise and sing ho - san - na!

HE IS RISEN

(A canon in 4 parts)

Arr. by Barbara Seaborn

Words and music by
Evelyn Minshull

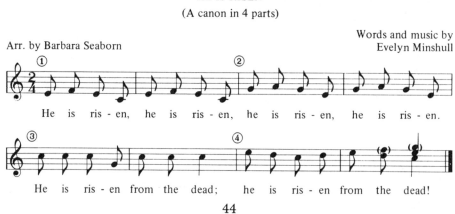

He is ris - en, he is ris - en, he is ris - en, he is ris - en.

He is ris - en from the dead; he is ris - en from the dead!

HOSANNA

(A canon in 4 parts)

Arr. by Barbara Seaborn

Evelyn Minshull

Ho - san-na, ho - san - na! Ho - san-na, ho - san - na!

Ho - san-na, ho-san-na, ho-san-na! Ho - san-na, ho-san-na, ho-san-na!

Ending:

Ho - san - na, ho - san - na!

HE IS RISEN

(A canon in 2 parts)

Arr. by Barbara Seaborn

Words and music by
Evelyn Minshull

He is ris - en; Je - sus Christ is ris - en.

(He is ris - en.) He is ris - en.

He is ris - en from the dead.

Je - sus Christ is ris - en. He is ris - en from the dead.

WHERE HAS THE LITTLE BABY GONE?

R. D. Townsend
D. L. Townsend

Where has the lit - tle ba - by gone?

1. He's left the man - ger bed. He looked so cute and
2. He's talk - ing to the wise. They mar - vel at his
3. He's preach - ing to the throng. They shout ho - san - na
4. He's hang - ing on a tree. They say it was the
5. He rose up from the grave. That lit - tle ba - by

in - no - cent with Ma - ry by his head.
know-ledge of the Fa - ther in the skies.
Lord and King as they fol - low him a - long.
plan of God that he die for you and me.
died and rose so that peo - ple could be saved.

Ho - san - na, ho - san - na, ho - san - na to the King,

Ho - san - na, ho - san - na, their joy - ful prais - es ring.

46

BITTER

J. E. Laird

CAPO 3
INTRO: 4m. Em sus, 4m. Em

1. Bit - ter bit - ter tears of an - guish stream-ing
Bit - ter burn - ing rain. Bit - ter
Bit - ter sor - row tears my bit - ter, burn- ing,
cry - ing heart of pain. I see him dy - ing
He's dy - ing. O God as you die
I die too, please take me with you.

2. Bitter–bitter death draws nearer
   Fading–fading life grows dim
   Bitter–bitter sorrow tears my bitter, burning, crying heart of pain.

   I see him dying
   He's dying.
   O God as you die I die, too
   Please take me with you.

LORD, WHY ME?

Words and music by
Barbara Seaborn

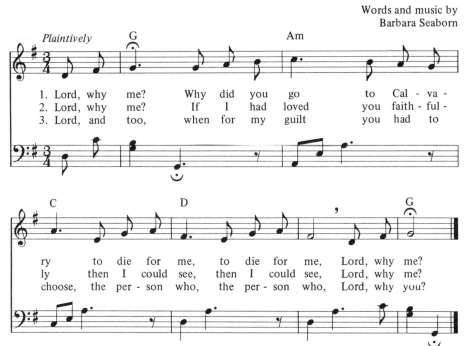

1. Lord, why me? Why did you go to Cal - va -
2. Lord, why me? If I had loved you faith - ful -
3. Lord, and too, when for my guilt you had to

ry to die for me, to die for me, Lord, why me?
ly then I could see, then I could see, Lord, why me?
choose, the per - son who, the per - son who, Lord, why you?

Note: This song should be sung as a solo by someone representing a disciple or other person in the crucifixion story, or a Christian today. Other verses may be added.

HOW EVER MANY DAYS

Arr. by Lillian Carnahan

Words and music by
Evelyn Minshull

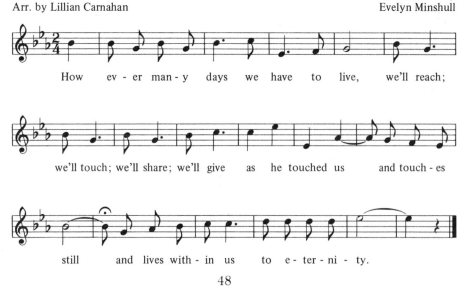

How ev - er man - y days we have to live, we'll reach;

we'll touch; we'll share; we'll give as he touched us and touch - es

still and lives with - in us to e - ter - ni - ty.